I KICK ASS AT WORK!

THE STRATEGY JOURNAL FOR CAREER PROFESSIONALS

by

SONIA ALLEYNE

Hunter Publishing Group titles are available at special quantity discounts for bulk purchases for sales promotion, premiums, fund-raising and educations or institutional use. To order, email info@hunterpublishinggroup.com

Hunter Publishing Group and the logo Reg. U.S. Pat. & TM Off.

Cover design by Iram shahzadi ("aaniyah.ahmed "99designs)

Interior Design by Iram shahzadi ("aaniyah.ahmed "99designs)

Edited by Chandra Sparks Taylor–www.chandrasparkstaylor.com

Stock Image(s): www.shutterstock.com

Stock Image: https://www.freepik.com/free-vector...825866.htm

Stock Image: https://www.freepik.com/free-vector...487501.htm

Author photo image: Felix Natal

First Hunter Publishing Group trade paperback printing 2020

For more information, or to contact the author, send correspondence to:

www.hunterpublishinggroup.com

Library of Congress Cataloging-in-Publication Data

ISBN-13: 0-9708191-6-1

ISBN-10: 1-7327002-3-0

10 9 8 7 6 5 4 3 2 1 First Paperback Edition

Printed in the United States of America

I KICK ASS AT WORK!

THE STRATEGY JOURNAL FOR CAREER PROFESSIONALS

I KICK ASS AT WORK!

A NEW PROFESSIONAL ATTITUDE

I was working as the consumer and lifestyle editor covering buying trends and lifestyle topics when I was offered the position of careers editor at the financial media company Black Enterprise Magazine. I took the job because I believed it would increase my profile as a writer and editor. I had no previous experience in creating content on career development, so while I was excited about this new opportunity, I was concerned about how successful I might be. How many stories can you really write about work? I thought: You look and interview for a job, you get hired for a job, you leave or lose the job. I had very simple and naïve ideas about what it took to advance in a profession.

I, like many other women, approached my career like I managed my schoolwork: If I studied, completed the assignments and did well on my exams, I would see the results of my hard work by receiving a good grade. Applying the same formula to my job—working hard and completing the assigned tasks—was supposed to yield similar results: promotions and higher salaries.

This new position, however, taught me that my attitude and ideas about career advancement were not just naïve and simple. This passive approach of working hard and waiting for results was crippling to any advancement goals. I was fortunate to have interviewed many senior-level executives, including a range of CEOs at some of the largest global corporations, such as Aetna, Xerox and McDonald's. I worked with some of corporate industry's most experienced career coaches and strategists on a broad range of topics to help our readers understand the difference between working hard and working smart, the unwritten and unspoken dynamics in the workplace and how our actions and attitudes about work assist in advancing and derailing careers.

As editorial director, I later helped develop the Black Enterprise Women of Power Summit, one of the first professional development conferences of its kind helping women create personal strategies for success in the workplace.

In the process of developing and introducing critical instruction on how to manage career growth, I realized that as young professionals, we weren't given the necessary tools or training to work smarter. The career advice that was often shared with young talent focused on the importance of people and interpersonal skills for better collaboration, productive teamwork and how to avoid conflict. We were told, "Abide by the rules, stay the course, and be a good team player." We weren't shown how to build support systems, manage our emotions or negotiate the culture of an organization to be able to advance our goals.

The popular business adage, "There is no I in team" encouraged a selfless approach to driving corporate success. Although teamwork is extremely important and necessary for completing many work tasks, it is also important that we focus on the "I's" that are in recognition, promotion—and the win, as basketball legend Michael Jordan famously noted about the no-I-in-team business proverb. Being recognized, increasing your salary and getting promoted are all important factors connected to winning in the workplace and advancing your professional goals.

Learning these new career advancement tactics and the nuances of how much workplace culture influences so many aspects of how we function on the job broadened my own personal awareness. It also heightened my level of frustration because I realized that because of the dynamics in my own work culture, if I didn't speak up—if I didn't advocate for myself—growth opportunities in terms of promotions and raises were going to continue to be elusive, so I eventually made an appointment to meet with the CEO.

"You want a seventeen percent increase?"

My boss' tone was incredulous as his fingers on his desk calculator furiously figured out the percentage impact on my salary. "That's a big increase," he responded.

"I know," I said, listing all of the assignments and responsibilities I had taken on over the years since joining the company. They were significant: I was managing and contributing to several new lines of revenue-generating businesses across multiple units.

"I haven't had a raise since I've taken on all of these new responsibilities," I argued. "These responsibilities have expanded into several departments across the company, and my salary and title haven't changed." I was angry, and I was clear if nothing changed, it would be time for me to find another job in a different organization.

"I'll look and see what we can do," he said dryly, "but Sonia, managing your career is your responsibility."

I remember feeling almost enraged by that response. I had outperformed in so many areas for this organization without financial recognition or a promotion. When all of my pent-up anger and frustration had finally driven me to ask for what I thought I deserved, I was told if I didn't feel I was treated fairly, well, that was my fault.

How dare you? I thought. I ended up getting the raise and a promotion, but I also learned a profound lesson that day. He was right.

Over the years, I have and continue to mentor many young women on their career paths, and I hear a lot of complaints about what mangers and organizations are not doing to support their goals and dreams. It is true, bosses can be difficult and companies can be challenging, but often employees have more power than they are willing to be accountable for. The real question is what are you doing to move your career to the next level. What are you doing that may be derailing your success? What are you doing that is causing stagnation?

Those are the questions I constantly ask my mentees as I help them find appropriate answers to their challenges at work. Those discussions have been the inspiration for this strategy journal, I Kick Ass at Work!

There are a number of great books and resources that offer corporate strategies and tactics for getting ahead. I have recommended them and even co-authored one, called Good Is Not Enough: And Other Unwritten Rules for Minority Professionals, but I wanted to provide a tool specifically for young women just starting out on their career path that encouraged them to consistently review their actions and demeanor at work. The late motivational speaker Wayne Dyer often said, "When you change the way you look at things, the things you look at change."

The purpose of this journal is to help you change the way you look at your job and direct your attention to changing behaviors and thought patterns so that you will enhance your performance and stay focused on your career goals.

For me, it is not a coincidence that the acronym for I Kick Ass at Work (IKAAW), in Filipino (spelled with one "a"), is a pronoun that means singular you.

Business organizations are complicated and intense workplaces. Although corporations have made tremendous strides in diversity, protecting Equal Employment Opportunities and creating programs that develop talent and improve retention, their goal is not to determine the appropriate trajectory for individual employees. What companies understand, however, is that there will be star players, average players and employees who will resign, or be fired, retired or laid off.

If you're going to succeed on your job as a star player, you'd better be kicking ass at work every day—and be confident in your ability to consistently do so. Today's corporate environment is fast–paced and results–oriented, driven by a globally competitive market, ever-changing technology and bottom–line economics. That's the foundational structure of business 2.0.

When you're starting out in your career, your job may seem like a very small part of the larger business matrix, but the skills and talents you develop at that level will be your foundation for bigger opportunities ahead. In the meantime, work is a seemingly never-ending series of managing projects and meeting deadlines for your units or divisions. While you are focused on executing deliverables, it is very easy to become so absorbed in achieving the manager's goals that you forget your own. There are also a number of factors—directly and indirectly connected to your job—that will influence your overall performance:

- Managers: Whether they are productive or ineffective, you still have to report to one. It is one of the most important relationships you'll ever have to manage in the workplace. A manager will direct your projects, complete your performance reviews and make recommendations that can advance or impede your trajectory at work. A major part of your job responsibility is to develop a relationship that will satisfy the demands of your supervisor as well as support your growth and development in that role.

- Associates: Most corporations are comprised of divisions and units with offices in different parts of the city, country and/or the world. Your unit may also have clients and/or partners who are connected to different firms or businesses. In large corporations, there is the opportunity to interact with a broad range of professionals, but even in smaller offices, interpersonal dynamics are always in play. The people with whom you work may have different ideas and values. They will also have different work styles and approaches to completing tasks. They will be part of your units. They will be project partners. Among them, you will find supporters, friends, competitors and backstabbers. Those relationships can also change over time because of the restructuring of a unit or a change in management. Sometimes you will happily coexist with your co-workers, but there will be times when you are disappointed or even enraged by their interactions with you on the job.

- Culture: One of the reasons employees struggle in an organization is not because they can't perform assigned duties. It's often because they don't understand the culture, or the values of the organization are not in alignment with the individual's personal values. The culture of an organization is defined by the unwritten rules of how the organization functions. It's not what you find in the "About Us" section of the website or the employee manual. It's the spirit of the company. It's not what the company does, but the manner in which they do it: What type of performance gets rewarded? Who tends to get promotions? What areas of business get the most attention and financial support? What are the company ethics? You can't even begin to map out a strategy for success until you understand the culture of your organization.

- Office Politics: This is very much aligned with the culture of the organization. You are obviously not the only one in your company with a goal for advancement. Your colleagues are also eyeing better opportunities. Some of your coworkers are fair and comprehensive in their strategies for promotions. Others are cutthroat and divisive. Your job is to find the tactics for navigating workplace games, while executing a strategy that advances your goals. You don't have to play dirty or nasty, but office politics do exist, and if you're interested in advancing in your company you've got to plan a strategy for how you intend to engage.

- Managing Emotions: This is probably one of the most difficult areas to negotiate. Mindset is everything. My grandmother used to say to me that she could work with the devil in hell. As a child, I struggled with its meaning. As an adult, I clearly get it: She meant that it didn't matter who she encountered, it would never set her off course. She would never allow someone else's demeanor or attitude to influence or alter her behavior. It is the most valuable lesson she ever taught me, and I try to operate in every aspect of my life from that mindset. Actions taken against us in the workplace always feel personal, but it's important to not allow your emotions to dictate your behavior. Your emotions should be used as a compass to uncover why you feel angry, hurt or discriminated against, but you should never make decisions or react to situations based on raw emotion.

When we are uncertain of how to manage these areas of our work life, we can easily become frustrated and begin to engage in counterproductive behavior: complaining and blaming others or the organization, doubting our capabilities, and becoming stagnant.

The following sections of I Kick Ass at Work!: The Strategy Journal for Career Professionals will provide guidance and direction to help strengthen your approach to building your career with strategies, tips, journaling instructions and inspirational coaching to help you kick ass at work!

WHY A CAREER JOURNAL?

Professional journaling serves two purposes:

- It provides invaluable insight and perspective: Writing is a spiritual, cathartic process for examining your thoughts and actions. It is a success strategy used by many prominent professionals. More than simply declaring or posting your goal, journaling is a tool that can help you examine your behavior, assess your performance and provide a safe space to question and vent. Expressing your thoughts, ideas, goals, frustrations and dilemmas on paper helps you objectively evaluate strengths and weaknesses, as well as the emotions that are connected to them. It provides the clarity and perspective you will need to address the necessary changes to advance your career to the next level.

- It provides an accurate and up-to-date record of achievement. The other important benefit of this strategy journal is to make your résumé and LinkedIn profile living documents and a current and accurate representation of your work. It is extremely important to document all of your achievements because everything you accomplish at work may not be recognized by your organization. These achievements, however, contribute to your abilities and talents as a professional. Also, unfortunately, most people only update résumés and LinkedIn profiles when they are presented with an opportunity or are thinking about pursuing a new one. In the haste, the details of your accomplishments are not always readily available by memory, which means they may not be properly documented. This journal allows for you to keep all of your achievements detailed in one place so you can accurately showcase your professional story to access the best opportunities.

HOW TO USE THIS JOURNAL?

Reflect on the kick-ass strategies, kick-ass tips and inspirational quotes. These are quotes, tips and strategies I have shared with readers and mentees over the years. Many of the quotes are strategies from very successful professionals working at the highest levels in business. The content throughout this journal was selected because it focuses on what you can personally do to change or enhance how you work. These strategies will help guide you professionally in every area of your career and help shape your work habits.

Use it regularly. Make it a habit to regularly review and update your goals. Record your successes, failures, challenges and lessons as frequently as they occur. It will help you accurately determine your progress. The truth is, the more time passes, the less details you remember about what you've experienced or achieved, the impact it has had on your company, and the significance of what you've learned.

Be specific. When recording in your journal, provide detail. This is a private and safe space to brag, vent and truly expound on work experiences. For your successes, don't just note, "Awarded top salesperson for the month." Write, "Bringing in $10 million, I was awarded top salesperson of the month. That amount was $5 million more than the second-highest salesperson and ten percent more than my division's goal for the month. I beat my personal goal by five percent."

RECORD, REVIEW, REFLECT and RESOLVE:

A Working Process for Success Kicking ass at work is a professional attitude of personal power and confidence that aligns with corporate expectations. This journal, through process of Record, Review, Reflect and Resolve is designed to help you refocus your attention and strategies on your personal successes by recording your individual work activity and scenarios, reviewing their impact on your goals, reflecting on what changes need to be made and then focusing on a resolution to enhance your effectiveness.

Using this journal consistently to document your thoughts, feelings and achievements will help you better assess your attitude toward work and your level of performance. As a result, it will prompt you to make adjustments in real time to keep your career objectives in focus.

This journal provides a dedicated space for your professional goals and the strategies to get you there. It will help you focus less on the challenges of workplace drama and more on how you can manage your responses to it by staying mindful of the narrative you want to design for your professional journey

Record. To be able to accurately tell your professional story, you have to record it. Keep a detailed, up-to-date record of your accomplishments and achievements. Outline the lessons you've learned, how you might have executed tasks differently, and the impact this success has on team dynamics in your unit, division and the overall company.

Review. To be able to change your behavior, you have to review your thoughts and actions. Examine or assess challenges, breakthroughs and opportunities with the intention of enhancing and/or changing how you perform at work. Gauge your progress over time and note gains as well as stagnation.

Reflect. Reflecting on your behavior and responses gives you the perspective you need to make changes. Ask yourself questions about why you continue to engage the same way and why certain situations continue to elicit the same feelings. Reflection will help you notice patterns of behavior that should be improved or discarded.

Resolve. Once you recognize patterns or responses that do not serve your goals for advancement, you have to make changes. The resolution section of the journal is where you will make notes for revisions and adjustments. It is also important to reinforce those behaviors and thought patterns that provide favorable outcomes toward your goals.

Benefits of Using the 4R's

Allows you to maintain an accurate, up-to-date record of your accomplishments and achievements and make updates to your résumé and LinkedIn profile.

- You can examine your emotional and practical career patterns around your work history in order to make smarter decisions about what needs to be changed or enhanced.

- You are better prepared during your work evaluations with your manager by being able to discuss the details of your work for better feedback.

- Offers you the chance to record important information—whether it was something you read or discussed in a meeting that will impact your approach to work.

- Helps you be deliberate and accountable in the part you play in reaching your goals or sabotaging them.

I KICK ASS AT WORK!

GETTING STARTED

Career development is a growth process. Each new task, project and job will expand your experience as well as build and strengthen your skill sets. It is important that you have a clear understanding of what you do well, what you need to improve and what you need to learn in order to reach your goals. The information you provide in this first section will help you assess your baseline status as you begin to set the framework and foundation for your professional journey.

ACKNOWLEDGE YOUR TALENTS

Even if you don't have a breadth of work experience, you should feel confident in the talents you possess. Talents are natural abilities that allow you to define yourself uniquely in the workplace. It is an adeptness that you own and apply to every work situation. Talents include important and valuable strengths such as problem solving, working well with diverse groups of people, public speaking, critical thinking, communicating well, identifying trends, etc. Being able to identify your talents will be a vital part of constructing your professional narrative.

TAKE **YOUR TIME** AND LIST ALL OF THE **TALENTS** THAT HAVE CURRENTLY OR COULD **ENHANCE** YOUR **PERFORMANCE** IN THE **WORKPLACE:**

1. ______________________________

____

2. ______________________________

____

3. ______________________________

____

4. ______________________________

____

5. ______________________________

____

6. ______________________________

____

7. ______________________________

____

8. ______________________________

____

9. ______________________________

____

10______________________________

____

LIST YOUR SKILLS

Skills are learned and developed abilities. They are specific to job performance and measured by how you perform. For example, if you worked as a corporate event planner, your skills would include everything required to plan and execute an event, such as managing a budget, negotiating contracts, booking appropriate venues and managing special guests and attendees. The success of the event would be the measurement of your skill level. Were you able to come in under budget? Were you able to negotiate a good deal? Was the content well received by attendees? How you perform will determine how you access opportunities, the salary you command and your reputation in your company and in your respective industry.

HERE YOU WILL **MAKE** TWO LISTS - **SKILLS YOU HAVE** AND SKILLS YOU'D LIKE TO **IMPROVE** OR **ACQUIRE.**

CURRENT SKILL SET

1. ____
____

2. ____
____

3. ____
____

4. ____
____

5. ____
____

6. ____
____

7. ____
____

8. ____
____

9. ____
____

10____
____

FUTURE SKILL SET

1. ______________________________

____

2. ______________________________

____

3. ______________________________

____

4. ______________________________

____

5. ______________________________

____

6. ______________________________

____

7. ______________________________

____

8. ______________________________

____

9. ______________________________

____

10______________________________

____

CURRENT DEGREES AND PROFESSIONAL CERTIFICATES

HERE, YOU WILL **LIST THE DETAILS** OF ANY **DEGREES** AND/OR **PROFESSIONAL CERTIFICATES** INCLUDING **SPECIAL HONORS, INSTITUTIONS, DATES** AND **LOCATIONS.**

1. ____

____

____

____

2. ____

____

____

____

3. ____

____

____

____

4. ____

____

____

____

5. ____

____

____

____

FUTURE DEGREES AND PROFESSIONAL CERTIFICATES

Improving your skill set should be an ongoing goal for you as you aspire to grow and develop in your profession. It will be your competitive advantage in the workforce. Some jobs require advanced degrees; others may require advanced learning or a more comprehensive knowledge of industry dynamics.

AFTER YOU HAVE **DETERMINED** WHAT MAY BE REQUIRED FOR YOUR **CAREER GOALS** AND **ASPIRATIONS,** LIST THE DEGREES AND/OR **PROFESSIONAL CERTIFICATES/**COURSES YOU WOULD LIKE TO ACQUIRE.

1. ____

____

____

____

2. ____

____

____

____

3. ____

____

____

____

4. ____

____

____

____

5. ____

____

____

____

SETTING A DIRECTIONAL PATH

Working as an editor, I had several opportunities to interview professionals in the auto racing industry. I also was fortunate enough to enjoy track racing and defensive driving with several major auto brands. Although each had its own appeal and attractions, each driving instructor offered the same advice: Where you focus your eyes while you're in the car is where you'll go. They said the reason there are so many roadside accidents involving poles and trees is that in a driving crisis, most people focus on the thing they are trying to avoid instead of looking where they would like to direct the car. That was such a perfect metaphor on the importance of operating with a destination in mind.

Goals are where you set your vision so you are not distracted—so you don't crash. For your journey, you will also need instructors who will help you navigate the course. This section asks you to outline four sets of career objectives: What you'd like to accomplish in the next three months, in the next six months, in one year and in the next five years. It also provides a space to identify mentors and advisors to help you along the way.

MY PERSONAL ADVISORY BOARD

Every successful professional has benefitted from the instruction and guidance of mentors and advisors inside and outside of their organization. They can be found at various professional levels, but they are people whom you trust will give you critical feedback and advise you on how best to handle people and situations at work. Many corporations have formal mentorship programs where they assign senior employees to work with selected mentees. Whether your company has such a program, know that mentorship can also happen more organically. In every new work environment, you should identify a person or persons to serve as your mentor(s). They should be people who are successful, respected in their roles and, most importantly, understand the culture of the organization. They will often help with work and life strategies to help you navigate the dynamics in your current company. Don't be discouraged if a prospective mentor turns you down. Mentorship is a mutual commitment, and a good mentor will make the time to work with you. It is also important that you are respectful of that investment of time and be just as diligent at managing the relationship.

Advisors are professionals who are senior in position, but can help you with very specific guidance based on their own expertise and level of success. They are able to give you play-by-play instruction to help move you to the next level. Mentors and advisors will want to work with someone they feel has potential, is dedicated, disciplined and will follow the advice they offer. Being fully engaged and committed will be

A VITAL PART OF HOW MUCH YOU **BENEFIT** FROM THESE **RELATIONSHIPS.** WHO'S ON YOUR TEAM? CREATE A LIST OF THOSE YOU'D LIKE TO **ENROLL** IN **YOUR SUCCESS.**

1. ____

____

2. ____

____

3. ____

____

4. ____

____

5. ____

____

6. ____

____

7. ____

____

8. ____

____

9. ____

____

10____

____

WHAT I EXPECT TO ACHIEVE IN THREE MONTHS

TODAY'S DATE:

Here, it's important to set easily attainable goals to lay the foundation of your growth, and so you can start to feel empowered. Goals may include more regularly scheduled meetings with your supervisor to improve feedback and direction, organizing your workspace, identifying mentors, setting up lunch dates with a certain number of people in your network, and updating your résumé and LinkedIn profile.

WHAT I EXPECT TO ACHIEVE IN SIX MONTHS

TODAY'S DATE:

For the next set of goals, you may want to stretch a little. Identify promotional tracks in your company or courses, training or a degree to expand your skill set. Join a professional organization, or if you are already a member, apply for a leadership role. Solidify at least two mentors—one inside your company and one in your industry outside of your organization.

WHAT I EXPECT TO ACHIEVE IN IN ONE YEAR

TODAY'S DATE:

In a year, you want to see movement. Your goals should be centered on growth and change. You will have enrolled in or completed a course, a class or training program. You will have a new title, a new role, or be in a new company, or maybe you will have signed up for an overseas assignment.

WHAT I EXPECT TO ACHIEVE IN THE NEXT FIVE YEARS

TODAY'S DATE:

Dream and be specific in your declarations. What company would you like to work for and what position do you want? What is your work environment like? How much money are you earning? How many people are you managing? What type of industry leader are you? How are you impacting and driving change?

WHAT ARE YOU WILLING TO RISK?

All successful business professionals have taken risks in their careers. Taking a risk requires you to step outside of your comfort zone. You don't ever want to be reckless, but you will have to stretch beyond what seems safe and familiar. Calculated risks are where you've weighed the options and have determined the benefits and possible disadvantages. Risk taking also requires a serious gut check. You may seek guidance and direction from your mentors, advisors, family and friends, but at the end of it all, you'll also have to trust your intuition. There are some areas at work where risk is not an option. For example, if you work in the medical field, anything that may put a person's life in jeopardy is not a risk option. Applying for a management position that unexpectedly opened up after evaluating the pros and cons of your application, however, may be a risk worth taking.

BELOW ARE **TWO SECTIONS** TO **HELP** YOU **DETERMINE NO-RISK** AREAS OF WORK AND **RISK POSSIBILITIES.**

AREAS OF WORK WHERE THERE IS NO COMPROMISE

1. ______________________________

2. ______________________________

3. ______________________________

4. ______________________________

5. ______________________________

RISK POSSIBILITIES

1. Risk

Benefit | Challenges

2. Risk

Benefit | Challenges

3. Risk

Benefit | Challenges

4. Risk

Benefit | Challenges

5. Risk

Benefit | Challenges

KNOW YOUR COMPANY CULTURE

I KICK ASS STRATEGIES

Culture in an organization dictates how that company operates—its ideology, protocol and etiquette. It is representative of what the organization values. Corporate culture is less about what a company says about itself and more about how it actually functions. Sometimes it's apparent and clear. Other times, it's less obvious. Mentors, sponsors and advisors inside an organization are key in helping decode its culture. Here's why you have to understand the rules of engagement.

- Culture determines what success looks like in your organization. What gets rewarded? What are the priority functions—sales, operations, marketing? Who gets promoted? Culture also influences social activities. Do team members regularly meet for drinks after work or like to celebrate after completing a major assignment?

- When employees fail, it usually isn't because they can't do the work. They fail because they don't fit into the culture or don't understand how the culture impacts the work environment. Fitting in is a choice, but you have to know what you are choosing before you can decide if this organization is best suited for your career trajectory.

When you understand the culture, you can strategically set goals that are in alignment with goals of the organization. Understanding that it's not a fit alleviates the feelings of frustration and empowers you to look for new opportunities.

ATTRACT A SPONSOR

Earlier in the section, "My Personal Advisory Board," you were asked to identify and list professionals you would like to guide you on your professional journey. These are the mentors and advisors who will provide important information and direction about your work performance, attitude and interactions with bosses and colleagues. These "counselors" will help you manage how you function at work. Sponsors actually help advance you in your career. If your goal is to eventually reach the C-Suite, you will need a sponsor to help get you there. One significant difference between the two types of support is that you choose your mentors and advisors; sponsors choose you. Here's what you need to know in order to attract one.

- Sponsors are unique in that they are senior-level executives who can influence the direction of your career. They speak and negotiate on your behalf when you are not in the room when important decisions are made that can impact your position in the company.

- Sponsors support star players—high-performing employees who show potential for leadership positions.

- Sponsors can help break racial and gender-related workplace barriers because they use their network and influence to support and position the employees, they believe in.

BUILD AND STRENGTHEN YOUR NETWORK

Your professional network of colleagues and associates is important for many reasons: The people in your network furnish valuable information about your company and industry, and they provide leads to new opportunities. More than 85 percent of all job offers come from relationships in your network, so it's important to find ways to strengthen how you engage with professional friends, colleagues and associates. These relationships must be nurtured and maintained. It's a lot easier to ask a favor of someone with whom you've been in touch instead of calling only when you need a favor. Here are a few ways to keep your network engaged and the conversation going:

- Schedule dates to meet colleagues, associates and professional friends for lunch, dinner or a cup of coffee.
- Remember their birthdays and/or special occasions, and reach out to them with a note of congratulations.
- Send relevant and important information to an associate with a note that you were thinking of them. It could be news related to their company and/or industry or information on a hobby or social activity connected to their interests.

When possible, make introductions that connect professionals in your network who have like interests or similar goals. For example, if a colleague relocates to a town where you have several connections that may, in some way, be helpful, make an email introduction to connect them.

ENGAGE AT EVERY STAGE

Don't wait for formal performance reviews to seek feedback from your manager. Depending on the organization, performance reviews may be conducted a few times a year—not often enough to provide important feedback to help you perform at optimal levels. Regular conversations that provide specific and critical information on your performance will greatly improve how you function at work. There are several reasons why you should make checking in with your supervisor an active part of your relationship:

- It gives you an immediate assessment of how you execute tasks so you can make the necessary changes on future tasks and projects.
- It encourages your supervisor to provide critical feedback he or she might not have volunteered worrying you might feel offended or insulted.
- It encourages a more collaborative and trusting working relationship with your supervisor.
- It shows you're engaged and interested in making sure projects are successfully executed.

CONSTANTLY REASSESS YOUR COMPANY

Just as your company does annual evaluations of its employees by determining its star players for promotion and where they will be making cuts in the organization, it's important that you regularly assess your company to determine its competitiveness and relevance in the marketplace—and if it continues to support your professional goals. These are questions to consider:

- Is your company a global organization? If it isn't, will global experience be an important factor for your career goals?
- Is your company a leader in industry trends or is it lagging? How are trade publications reporting on your company and companies like yours?
- Is your division being supported with all the necessary resources, or is it being streamlined? How are enhancements or reductions affecting your areas of responsibility?

I KICK ASS AT WORK!

DEVELOP AND MANAGE YOUR BRAND

There are entire books on personal and professional branding, but very simply put, your brand is the message you communicate about who you are through your actions and your attitude in the workplace. I like to say everyone has a brand—whether they like it or not, whether they know it or not. Your performance and your demeanor will determine how you are perceived by colleagues with whom you work and those who observe you. There are ways, even as a young professional to develop a strong and positive profile, particularly in the areas of work attendance, how well you perform, and your levels of interest and engagement:

- The time you show up for work can be a very simple yet defining way to make a statement about your commitment to your job. Getting into work early every day is a habit that managers will notice and appreciate, especially in times of an emergency or when they are interested in reviewing a situation before the day starts. Arriving late every day obviously sends a less positive message about your engagement level.

- How and when you complete assignments will brand your level of effectiveness and efficiency in a company. Are you ahead of deadlines or do you run late? Are you completing projects beyond the level of expectation or does your work always require follow-up from your manager? Strengthening your manager's team by working efficiently goes a long way in how your value is perceived.

- Don't confine your brand development to inside your company. Be active in professional organizations by volunteering your services in areas that showcase your talents and abilities. Also, consider blogging and posting articles about relevant topics on LinkedIn. It's a great way to connect with your online network by demonstrating your interests, knowledge and insight.

THINK LIKE AN ATHLETE

Once work environments become familiar and you find your rhythm in an organization, it's very easy to become complacent. Even when employees are dissatisfied with their surroundings, sometimes it is easier for many to function unhappily in what we're accustomed to than to risk change. Athletes are great professional roles models because of their high-performance levels and their attitudes about competing and overcoming adversity. They are never satisfied with being comfortable. They are trained to focus on winning and are willing to push themselves mentally and physically to achieve their goals. Here's what you could learn from top-performing sports professionals:

- They don't waver about winning. They are clear about what is expected of them and operate with an end goal in mind remaining steady and focused—even through challenges.

- They are constantly training, preparing mentally and physically to win. Even after a victory, they get refocused in order to improve their performance for the next game or competition.

- Failure is not defeat. It's a learning opportunity to be better, smarter, more strategic. It's a chance to redesign or restructure the game plan.

RULES OF THE GODFATHER

Several years ago, I interviewed Renetta McCann, who at the time was the CEO of Starcom MediaVest Group. She said the book The Godfather was one of the best books written on business. Don Vito Coreleon's character, although head of a mafia crime family, she argued, lived and ran his business operations by strong and effective principles that could be modeled by any legitimate business—or young professional. I have often shared these strategies with my mentees:

- He surrounded himself with good advisors. In this journal, that is one of your first assignments—identifying the people in your network who will become your advisors. They will be mentors and advisors who you will choose because of their positions in your company, their expertise and their willingness to help you advance your goals.

- He knew his opponents. For the young professional, this involves knowing the landscape of your organization. You will have colleagues with whom you work well, but there will sometimes be opponents and adversaries. It's important to know and understand all the players in your organization so you can create a strategy for managing these relationships.

- He worked quid pro quo. Working quid pro quo means he did favors for others, and as a result, expected favors in return. That is how our professional networks operate. It's the development and nurturing of relationships that are mutually beneficial to all involved. Your network should provide important information, as well as connections to new opportunities. It's hard to depend on that level of support from your network if you haven't made efforts to provide some support to colleagues and associates in your circle.

- He never made a move before his time. This speaks to being prepared. Your long-term goals will require a certain level of expertise—and possibly an additional degree or certification. You may feel anxious or impatient about the process, but if you focus on doing the work in alignment with your goals, you will increasingly feel confident as new opportunities present themselves.

- He never made decisions based on emotion. In the book The Godfather, there was one overly emotional character—Don Corleon's son, Sonny—who was eventually killed. You can never allow your emotions to be the driver of how you respond to slights, protocol changes or disagreements. This is not to say you aren't allowed to feel angry, jealous, resentful or any other strong emotion. It is absolutely necessary that you sit with your feelings and examine why they are affecting you in the way they do, but being reactionary clouds your judgment, which puts you at a disadvantage while you're processing what actions to take next.

STAY FOCUSED

One of the most important strategies for you to implement will be to stay focused on your goals and objectives. A mentor once told me that success is the result of performing at exceptional levels consistently over an extended period of time. To be able to maintain that level of excellence, you cannot allow yourself to be distracted by changing conditions or circumstances. As I've mentioned before, workplaces are dynamic organizations that are affected by the economy, changing consumer demands, competitive forces and management restructurings. Your job is to stay mindful of your goals and watchful of signs that may indicate a change in management operations.

- Set a mutually agreed upon schedule to meet with your mentors and advisors. Regular meetings mean that goals are constantly being discussed and reviewed, which keeps you focused on next steps for advancement.

- If offered a new position, take time to evaluate the benefits. Will this move you closer to your goals? If it is not connected to a future goal, will it, at least, allow you to stretch and develop new skills?

- Spend time researching industry trends by reading trade publications, attending conferences and connecting with professional groups. Staying ahead of the trends provides guidance on how to stay competitive and marketable.

THE JOURNAL

Here is where you will begin documenting experiences. The hardest part will be making this a dedicated practice of recording information, actions and attitudes that impact how you function in the workplace so you can regularly review and make the necessary changes to improve your performance on the job.

- After you write the date of entry, circle the experience you will be recording: Were you challenged by an event, situation or person at work? Did you learn a valuable lesson in a meeting, during an exchange or at a business conference? Did you have a win—a successful presentation, a compliment from management, a business connection?

- In the How Do I Feel About It? section, record your feelings about your experience: anger, resentment, excitement, anxiety, satisfaction, pride.

- The Resolution section is where you record how you have resolved the matter. Know that your resolution may not occur at the same time you record the experience and your feelings about it. It may come days, weeks, or even months after you've had time to review and reflect on its significance. Some experiences may not require a resolution at all. When you do record your resolution, write in the new date. This will help you track growth and perspective.

It's important to remember this is a safe place for you to honestly examine your exchanges with bosses and colleagues, your feelings about your abilities and how they translate in the workplace, as well as the level of excitement or dispassion you have for the type of work you do.

On these pages, you literally get to unload all the thoughts and emotions you carry around about your profession in one place. You get to look at it without judgment or penalty and make informed decisions of how you would like to enhance or redirect your professional journey.

I created this journal because I wanted women to feel empowered by their work, not burdened by it. As you move toward gaining more control over your career, consider the following intention or mantra in helping to create work experiences that will be fulfilling, rewarding and in line with your life's purpose.

I KICK ASS AT WORK!

WORK INTENTION

I am guided and protected in my work, and I perform my job accessing the best of my talents and abilities. I am innovative and creative, always finding solutions to perceived tough questions and challenging situations. I attract opportunities that advance me professionally and match my personal interests and principles. I am eternally grateful for the opportunity to pursue my passion and provide value in my organization and the community at large. I kick ass at work!

"THIS **POURING THOUGHTS** OUT ON PAPER HAS **RELIEVED** ME. I FEEL **BETTER** AND FULL OF **CONFIDENCE** AND **RESOLUTION.**"

DIET EMAN,
Author, *Things We Couldn't Say*
(on the importance of journaling)

I KICK ASS AT WORK!

TODAY'S DATE

CHALLENGE I LESSON I WIN (Circle one)

HOW DO I FEEL ABOUT IT?

RESOLUTION DATE

"You have to allow yourself to be in the space where you are carried by the flow of life and not pushing upstream. When you are in the flow, all things come as they should, all the time.

I BELIEVE YOU CAN **MOVE** INTO THE **STRATOSPHERE.** I BELIEVE **THERE IS NO CEILING."**

OPRAH WINFREY,
Media Executive,
Film and Television Producer

I KICK ASS AT WORK!

TODAY'S DATE

CHALLENGE I LESSON I WIN (Circle one)

HOW DO I FEEL ABOUT IT?

RESOLUTION DATE

KICK-ASS TIP

Invest in your career development. Attend professional development conferences and workshops.

HAVE YOUR **RÉSUMÉ PROFESSIONALLY** REDESIGNED AND CONSIDER HIRING A **CAREER COACH.**

I KICK ASS AT WORK!

TODAY'S DATE

CHALLENGE I LESSON I WIN (Circle one)

HOW DO I FEEL ABOUT IT?

RESOLUTION DATE

"There's usually no shortage of great ideas in organizations. Can you bring this idea from concept to execution, and what do you need to do in between thinking of the idea and making it work? That really comes down to knowing that the idea

IS **FEASIBLE,** THAT IT FITS WITHIN THE **STRATEGY** OF YOUR ORGANIZATION, THAT IT CAN BE **PROFITABLE,** AND THAT YOU CAN **OPERATIONALIZE** IT."

JERRI DEVARD,
EVP, Chief Customer Officer
at Office Depot

I KICK ASS AT WORK!

TODAY'S DATE

CHALLENGE I LESSON I WIN (Circle one)

HOW DO I FEEL ABOUT IT?

RESOLUTION DATE

KICK-ASS TIP

Passion is the exuberance you bring to your work. Emotion is the attachment to the outcome of that work. Passion brings satisfaction. Emotion, especially if it's internalized, brings frustration and stress.

KNOWING THE DIFFERENCE WILL **HELP** YOU **BETTER ACCESS** OPPORTUNITIES AND **MANAGE CHALLENGES** ON **THE JOB.**

I KICK ASS AT WORK!

TODAY'S DATE

CHALLENGE I LESSON I WIN (Circle one)

HOW DO I FEEL ABOUT IT?

RESOLUTION DATE

"Inspiration is an awareness of what you would like to have, what you would like to choose, what you would like to do—so it's a choice. Inspiration and fun are the same thing, but most folks don't make that connection.

WHEN YOU **CHOOSE** WHAT'S **FUN,** YOU ARE GOING TO **KEEP** BEING **INSPIRED."**

RICKY WILLIAMS,

Former American Football Running Back

I KICK ASS AT WORK!

TODAY'S DATE

CHALLENGE I LESSON I WIN (Circle one)

HOW DO I FEEL ABOUT IT?

RESOLUTION DATE

KICK-ASS TIP

Passion is the exuberance you bring to your work. Emotion is the attachment to the outcome of that work. Passion brings satisfaction. Emotion, especially if it's internalized, brings frustration and stress.

KNOWING THE **DIFFERENCE** WILL **HELP** YOU BETTER **ACCESS** OPPORTUNITIES AND **MANAGE** CHALLENGES ON **THE JOB.**

I KICK ASS AT WORK!

TODAY'S DATE

CHALLENGE I LESSON I WIN (Circle one)

HOW DO I FEEL ABOUT IT?

RESOLUTION DATE

KICK-ASS TIP

Stop getting emotional. If someone has disappointed you, take it as a gift. Now you know how they think and how they operate.

YOUR JOB **NOW** IS TO BE **SMARTER** ABOUT HOW YOU **INTERACT** WITH THEM.

I KICK ASS AT WORK!

TODAY'S DATE

CHALLENGE I LESSON I WIN (Circle one)

HOW DO I FEEL ABOUT IT?

RESOLUTION DATE

"LIVE YOUR **LIFE** BY **DESIGN**, **NOT BY DEFAULT."**

AUDRA BOHANNON,

Senior Partner,
Korn Ferry Hay Group

I KICK ASS AT WORK!

TODAY'S DATE

CHALLENGE I LESSON I WIN (Circle one)

HOW DO I FEEL ABOUT IT?

RESOLUTION DATE

KICK-ASS TIP

ALWAYS **ACT** WITH **INTEGRITY**- EVEN WHEN YOUR COLLEAGUES DON'T.

I KICK ASS AT WORK!

TODAY'S DATE

CHALLENGE I LESSON I WIN (Circle one)

HOW DO I FEEL ABOUT IT?

RESOLUTION DATE

"You've always got to ask yourself, 'How can I derive better performance over time?' The nature of business is to balance the things you need to deal with today against

WHERE YOU'RE **HEADED** AND HOW YOU'RE GOING TO GET THERE IN THE **FUTURE."**

WILLIAM PLUMMER,
Former Chief Financial Officer,
United Rentals

I KICK ASS AT WORK!

TODAY'S DATE

CHALLENGE I LESSON I WIN (Circle one)

HOW DO I FEEL ABOUT IT?

RESOLUTION DATE

KICK-ASS TIP

YOU MAY NOT HAVE **CONTROL** OF A **SITUATION,**

BUT YOU ALWAYS HAVE CONTROL OVER HOW YOU **RESPOND** TO IT.

I KICK ASS AT WORK!

TODAY'S DATE

CHALLENGE I LESSON I WIN (Circle one)

HOW DO I FEEL ABOUT IT?

RESOLUTION DATE

"Take risks. Without taking risks, you may get along, but you're [not] going to excel. You can't be afraid to move. I have no interest in being comfortable.

DON'T SHY AWAY FROM **CHALLENGES.** GO AFTER CHALLENGES. THE **PAYOFF** CAN BE **INCREDIBLE."**

MICHAEL TODMAN,
Former President,
Whirlpool International

I KICK ASS AT WORK!

TODAY'S DATE

CHALLENGE I LESSON I WIN (Circle one)

HOW DO I FEEL ABOUT IT?

RESOLUTION DATE

KICK-ASS TIP

LEAVE **REGRETS** FOR **YESTERDAY** AND **PROMISES** FOR **TOMORROW.** WHAT ARE YOU DOING TODAY TO **FULFILL** YOUR **DREAMS, GOALS** AND **DESIRES?**

I KICK ASS AT WORK!

TODAY'S DATE

CHALLENGE I LESSON I WIN (Circle one)

HOW DO I FEEL ABOUT IT?

RESOLUTION DATE

"I REALIZED THAT I WAS MORE **CONVINCING** TO **MYSELF** AND TO THE PEOPLE WHO WERE **LISTENING** WHEN I ACTUALLY SAID WHAT I **THOUGHT,** VERSUS WHAT

I THOUGHT **PEOPLE** WANTED TO **HEAR ME** SAY."

URSULA BURNS,
Chairman of VEON

I KICK ASS AT WORK!

TODAY'S DATE

CHALLENGE I LESSON I WIN (Circle one)

HOW DO I FEEL ABOUT IT?

RESOLUTION DATE

KICK-ASS TIP

Stop eating lunch at your desk because you feel you don't have the time to take a break. Plan to meet a colleague or a new contact for a meal or a cup of coffee. Make strengthening your professional relationships a priority. Statistics continue to show that roughly 85 percent of new opportunities come through a personal network.

MAKE THE **TIME** TO **BETTER DEVELOP** YOUR **CONNECTIONS.**

I KICK ASS AT WORK!

TODAY'S DATE

CHALLENGE I LESSON I WIN (Circle one)

HOW DO I FEEL ABOUT IT?

RESOLUTION DATE

"WE'RE ALWAYS **COMPLAINING** ABOUT WHAT IS **NOT HAPPENING,** BUT RARELY DO WE LOOK AT WHAT WE CAN **DO DIFFERENTLY** AND WHAT WE CAN **OWN.** IT REALLY ISN'T ABOUT WHAT HAPPENS TO YOU, IT'S HOW YOU **RESPOND."**

MICHAEL HYTER,
Senior Client Partner and Office Managing Director, Korn Ferry

I KICK ASS AT WORK!

TODAY'S DATE

CHALLENGE I LESSON I WIN (Circle one)

HOW DO I FEEL ABOUT IT?

RESOLUTION DATE

KICK-ASS TIP

RESTLESSNESS IS A **SIGN** THAT IT'S TIME TO **MOVE** OR MAKE A **CHANGE** IN WHAT **YOU** ARE DOING.

I KICK ASS AT WORK!

TODAY'S DATE

CHALLENGE I LESSON I WIN (Circle one)

HOW DO I FEEL ABOUT IT?

RESOLUTION DATE

"BOUNDARIES?
WHAT BOUNDARIES?
PRETEND THEY
DON'T EXIST.

THAT'S RIGHT, JUST
IGNORE THEM."

RENETTA MCCANN,
Chief Inclusion Experiences Officer,
Publicis Groupe

I KICK ASS AT WORK!

TODAY'S DATE

CHALLENGE I LESSON I WIN (Circle one)

HOW DO I FEEL ABOUT IT?

RESOLUTION DATE

KICK-ASS TIP

THE **EXPERIENCE** YOU GAIN IN YOUR CURRENT JOB WILL **PREPARE** YOU FOR YOUR NEXT **OPPORTUNITY.** DON'T GET SIDETRACKED OR DISTRACTED BY **EXCHANGES** AND **ENCOUNTERS** THAT DON'T **SERVE THIS GOAL.**

I KICK ASS AT WORK!

TODAY'S DATE

CHALLENGE I LESSON I WIN (Circle one)

HOW DO I FEEL ABOUT IT?

RESOLUTION DATE

"EVERY **DECISION** YOU MAKE IS ABOUT **COURAGE**, UNLESS YOU'RE **SATISFIED** SITTING ON THE **SIDELINES.**"

TENA CLARK,
CEO/Chief Creative Officer,
DMI Music & Media Solutions

I KICK ASS AT WORK!

TODAY'S DATE

CHALLENGE I LESSON I WIN (Circle one)

HOW DO I FEEL ABOUT IT?

RESOLUTION DATE

KICK-ASS TIP

EVERY **BATTLE** IS NOT A **WAR.**

I KICK ASS AT WORK!

TODAY'S DATE

CHALLENGE I LESSON I WIN (Circle one)

HOW DO I FEEL ABOUT IT?

RESOLUTION DATE

"YOU ARE **RESPONSIBLE** FOR YOUR OWN **SUCCESS.** NOT YOUR BOSS, NOT YOUR MENTOR, NOT YOUR COLLEAGUES. ONLY YOU CAN **'SELL'** YOURSELF **BEST.** LEARN TO SELL YOUR BRAND, AND FOR CRYING OUT LOUD, HAVE A **POINT OF VIEW.** DON'T SWAY WITH POPULAR OPINION.

TAKE A **STAND** AND **OWN** IT."

JENNY ALONZO,
CEO and Executive Producer,
Konation Media

I KICK ASS AT WORK!

TODAY'S DATE

CHALLENGE I LESSON I WIN (Circle one)

HOW DO I FEEL ABOUT IT?

RESOLUTION DATE

KICK-ASS TIP

IF YOU ARE **WILLING** TO **CHANGE** YOUR **PERSPECTIVE** ABOUT A SITUATION, YOU CAN **ALTER** HOW IT **AFFECTS** YOU.

I KICK ASS AT WORK!

TODAY'S DATE

CHALLENGE I LESSON I WIN (Circle one)

HOW DO I FEEL ABOUT IT?

RESOLUTION DATE

"Bringing the real you to work allows you to be free! Free to learn new concepts, free to be creative and responsive, free to take risks—all of which helps to enhance the professional that you are and makes you valuable to the organization. In today's competitive environment, the person who learns new concepts quickly, who can adapt commercially, or, in other words, can apply those lessons in a way that can make money for the firm, and who is also client-oriented,

IS THE **PERSON** WHO **MOVES** MOST **QUICKLY** IN A COMPANY AND IS **MOST** HANDSOMELY **REWARDED."**

CARLA HARRIS,

Vice Chairman of Wealth Management and Senior Client Advisor at Morgan Stanley and author of *Expect to Win*

I KICK ASS AT WORK!

TODAY'S DATE

CHALLENGE I LESSON I WIN (Circle one)

HOW DO I FEEL ABOUT IT?

RESOLUTION DATE

KICK-ASS TIP

MAKE SURE THE **INFORMATION** ON YOUR **LINKEDIN** PROFILE **MATCHES** WHAT IS ON YOUR **RÉSUMÉ.** DON'T **UPDATE** ONE WITHOUT THE OTHER.

I KICK ASS AT WORK!

TODAY'S DATE

CHALLENGE I LESSON I WIN (Circle one)

HOW DO I FEEL ABOUT IT?

RESOLUTION DATE

"YOU HAVE TO **ASK YOURSELF**, WHEN IS THE **FEEDBACK** YOU GET REALLY DATA THAT CAN **HELP ME**, AND WHEN IS IT JUST OPINION?"

AUDRA BOHANNON,

Senior Partner,
Korn Ferry Hay Group

I KICK ASS AT WORK!

TODAY'S DATE

CHALLENGE I LESSON I WIN (Circle one)

HOW DO I FEEL ABOUT IT?

RESOLUTION DATE

KICK-ASS TIP

In an adversarial situation, manage your emotions, present the facts, and ask the right questions. Emotional arguing puts you on the defensive.

USE SILENCE AS A **STRATEGY** TO BETTER **ANALYZE** THE INFORMATION AND **PROVIDE** APPROPRIATE **RESPONSES.**

I KICK ASS AT WORK!

TODAY'S DATE

CHALLENGE I LESSON I WIN (Circle one)

HOW DO I FEEL ABOUT IT?

RESOLUTION DATE

"IF YOU'RE **NOT MOVING UP**, YOU'RE EITHER WITH THE **WRONG** COMPANY OR WITH THE WRONG **BOSS.**"

JOYCE RUSSELL,
President, Adecco Staffing US

I KICK ASS AT WORK!

TODAY'S DATE

CHALLENGE I LESSON I WIN (Circle one)

HOW DO I FEEL ABOUT IT?

RESOLUTION DATE

KICK-ASS TIP

You have to ask for feedback that is specifically related to your tasks and responsibilities. Don't accept "It was good" or "That was fine" as responses to performance. Sometimes managers are afraid to offer critical assessments of work for fear of being accused of gender and/or racial bias.

BY **ASKING** FOR SPECIFIC **FEEDBACK,** YOU WILL RECEIVE THE INFORMATION YOU NEED TO **IMPROVE** YOUR **PERFORMANCE** AT WORK.

I KICK ASS AT WORK!

TODAY'S DATE

CHALLENGE I LESSON I WIN (Circle one)

HOW DO I FEEL ABOUT IT?

RESOLUTION DATE

"YOU **DISPEL** THE **MYTHS** BY PERFORMING BEYOND WHAT THE MYTH SAYS."

ROSALIND HUDNELL,

Former Vice President, Worldwide Corporate Affairs and President of Intel Foundation

I KICK ASS AT WORK!

TODAY'S DATE

CHALLENGE I LESSON I WIN (Circle one)

HOW DO I FEEL ABOUT IT?

RESOLUTION DATE

KICK-ASS TIP

Choose not to be reactionary or impulsive. Instead, be methodical, strategic and even engaging. It will enhance your performance, which in the end,

IS THE **ULTIMATE GAME CHANGER** ON THE JOB.

I KICK ASS AT WORK!

TODAY'S DATE

CHALLENGE I LESSON I WIN (Circle one)

HOW DO I FEEL ABOUT IT?

RESOLUTION DATE

"Hard work does pay off, but you must also be strategic in your choices and career path decisions. If you know you are consistently going above and beyond in your performance but you are not getting ahead,

YOU **NEED** TO TAKE **STOCK** OF THE SITUATION AND MAKE A **STRATEGIC DECISION.**"

JACKIE GLENN,
Diversity Executive

I KICK ASS AT WORK!

TODAY'S DATE

CHALLENGE I LESSON I WIN (Circle one)

HOW DO I FEEL ABOUT IT?

RESOLUTION DATE

KICK-ASS TIP

BRING ALL YOUR **EXPERIENCE,** BUT DON'T LET A LACK OF EXPERIENCE STOP YOU. IF YOU'RE **PRESENTED** WITH AN **OPPORTUNITY,** IT MEANS YOU'RE READY.

I KICK ASS AT WORK!

TODAY'S DATE

CHALLENGE I LESSON I WIN (Circle one)

HOW DO I FEEL ABOUT IT?

RESOLUTION DATE

"UNTIL YOU **LET IT GO,** YOU CAN'T LET IT COME IN. WHAT ARE YOU **UNWILLING** TO RELEASE THAT MAY BE **BLOCKING** YOUR **BLESSING?"**

SIMON BAILEY,
Author and Life Coach

I KICK ASS AT WORK!

TODAY'S DATE

CHALLENGE I LESSON I WIN (Circle one)

HOW DO I FEEL ABOUT IT?

RESOLUTION DATE

KICK-ASS TIP

MAKE SURE YOUR **PROFESSIONAL** GOALS ALIGN WITH YOUR ORGANIZATION'S **PRIORITIES** FOR BUSINESS GROWTH. IF THEY DON'T, CONSIDER THE WAYS YOU CAN **LEARN** AND **GROW** IN YOUR PRESENT ORGANIZATION UNTIL YOU FIND A COMPANY THAT WILL **SUPPORT YOUR GOALS.**

I KICK ASS AT WORK!

TODAY'S DATE

CHALLENGE I LESSON I WIN (Circle one)

HOW DO I FEEL ABOUT IT?

RESOLUTION DATE

"Make a decision! Leaders make decisions. Sometimes you'll have the luxury of time to analyze and other times you won't; some will be great and some will not.

BOTH **OUTCOMES CONSPIRE** TO MAKE YOU A **BETTER LEADER."**

JENNY ALONZO,
CEO and Executive Producer,
Konation Media

I KICK ASS AT WORK!

TODAY'S DATE

CHALLENGE I LESSON I WIN (Circle one)

HOW DO I FEEL ABOUT IT?

RESOLUTION DATE

KICK-ASS TIP

IT'S NOT **ALWAYS** WHO YOU **KNOW.** IT'S WHO KNOWS YOU. WHOSE LISTS ARE YOU ON?

I KICK ASS AT WORK!

TODAY'S DATE

CHALLENGE I LESSON I WIN (Circle one)

HOW DO I FEEL ABOUT IT?

RESOLUTION DATE

"THE WAY YOU **EMBRACE FEAR** OF FAILURE IS A BIG PART OF WHERE YOU END UP IN LIFE.

FAILURE FOR ME IS NOT TRYING."

SARA BLAKELY,
Creator, Spanx

I KICK ASS AT WORK!

TODAY'S DATE

CHALLENGE I LESSON I WIN (Circle one)

HOW DO I FEEL ABOUT IT?

RESOLUTION DATE

KICK-ASS TIP

TO BE **PROMOTED,** YOU HAVE TO KNOW WHAT **SUCCESS** LOOKS LIKE AND HOW IT IS **REWARDED** IN YOUR COMPANY.

I KICK ASS AT WORK!

TODAY'S DATE

CHALLENGE I LESSON I WIN (Circle one)

HOW DO I FEEL ABOUT IT?

RESOLUTION DATE

"The reason people fail at this is because they let others into their head. At this level, everybody's got an agenda. A friend on Monday is a foe on Tuesday.

I **DON'T** LET ANYBODY **MESS** WITH MY HEAD."

RENETTA MCCANN,
Chief Inclusion Experience Officer,
Publicis Groupe

I KICK ASS AT WORK!

TODAY'S DATE

CHALLENGE I LESSON I WIN (Circle one)

HOW DO I FEEL ABOUT IT?

RESOLUTION DATE

KICK-ASS TIP

PHYSICAL **TRAINING PREPARES** YOU FOR **PERFORMANCE.**

MENTAL **ATTITUDE PREPARES** YOU TO **WIN.**

I KICK ASS AT WORK!

TODAY'S DATE

CHALLENGE I LESSON I WIN (Circle one)

HOW DO I FEEL ABOUT IT?

RESOLUTION DATE

"GET MAD. THEN **GET OVER IT. FOES** CAN EVENTUALLY BECOME **ALLIES."**

COLIN POWELL,
Retired Four-Star General,
Former Secretary of State and
Author of *13 Rules of Leadership*

I KICK ASS AT WORK!

TODAY'S DATE

CHALLENGE I LESSON I WIN (Circle one)

HOW DO I FEEL ABOUT IT?

RESOLUTION DATE

KICK-ASS TIP

DON'T EXPECT MORE THAN YOUR COMPANY/ MANAGER IS CAPABLE OF GIVING.

DON'T WORK IN HOPE OF **WHAT'S NOT AVAILABLE.**

I KICK ASS AT WORK!

TODAY'S DATE

CHALLENGE I LESSON I WIN (Circle one)

HOW DO I FEEL ABOUT IT?

RESOLUTION DATE

"We can choose to be mediocre or to let others limit our lives, or we can choose to find out just how great we can be. That's a choice. If you really want to be an officer for a company,

YOU HAVE TO **CHOOSE** A **STRATEGY** THAT'S GOING TO **HELP** YOU **GET THERE."**

MICHAEL HYTER,
Senior Client Partner
and Office Managing Director,
Korn Ferry

I KICK ASS AT WORK!

TODAY'S DATE

CHALLENGE I LESSON I WIN (Circle one)

HOW DO I FEEL ABOUT IT?

RESOLUTION DATE

KICK-ASS TIP

WORKING HARD MEANS YOU GET A LOT DONE FOR YOUR COMPANY. WORKING SMART MEANS YOUR COMPANY DOES A LOT FOR **YOUR CAREER.**

I KICK ASS AT WORK!

TODAY'S DATE

CHALLENGE I LESSON I WIN (Circle one)

HOW DO I FEEL ABOUT IT?

RESOLUTION DATE

"Ambivalence is one of the biggest advancement obstacles. If you're not ambivalent, you're more focused and more disciplined because you can see what it is that you want.

IF YOU'RE **AMBIVALENT,** THE **ENERGY** AROUND, 'SHOULD I OR SHOULDN'T I?' **SLOWS YOU DOWN."**

AUDRA BOHANNON,
Senior Partner,
Korn Ferry

I KICK ASS AT WORK!

TODAY'S DATE

CHALLENGE I LESSON I WIN (Circle one)

HOW DO I FEEL ABOUT IT?

RESOLUTION DATE

KICK-ASS TIP

SOMETIMES WE **SPEND** MORE **TIME PREPARING** THAN DOING.

I KICK ASS AT WORK!

TODAY'S DATE

CHALLENGE I LESSON I WIN (Circle one)

HOW DO I FEEL ABOUT IT?

RESOLUTION DATE

"Far too many people take the next job just to 'climb the ladder.' In considering the next step, follow your heart, but use your head. Know yourself well enough to know what will make you excited, energized and engaged by the next move. If you do so, you will end up in the right place for you.

YOU WILL LIKELY **BE HAPPIER** AND ULTIMATELY MORE **SUCCESSFUL,** AND YOU WILL NOT FALL VICTIM TO OTHER PEOPLE'S OR EVEN YOUR OWN VIEWS OF WHAT YOU SHOULD DO AND BE."

JAMES GANDRE,
President,
Manhattan School of Music

I KICK ASS AT WORK!

TODAY'S DATE

CHALLENGE I LESSON I WIN (Circle one)

HOW DO I FEEL ABOUT IT?

RESOLUTION DATE

KICK-ASS TIP

Fear can be disguised in logic that makes you feel good about inaction. Your spirit, though, never lets you off that easily. Tap into what you are really feeling.

DON'T LET **FEAR STOP** YOU FROM **EXPLORING** AND **ACCESSING** NEW **OPPORTUNITIES.**

I KICK ASS AT WORK!

TODAY'S DATE

CHALLENGE I LESSON I WIN (Circle one)

HOW DO I FEEL ABOUT IT?

RESOLUTION DATE

"If you aspire to be with an organization, know how it makes its money, how it serves the customer base and how it works internally.

IF YOUR **FIRST RESPONSE** IS THAT YOU'RE NOT SURE IF YOU WANT TO BE HERE, YOU'VE ALREADY **LOST THE GAME."**

DON THOMPSON,
Founder and CEO of
Cleveland Avenue

I KICK ASS AT WORK!

TODAY'S DATE

CHALLENGE I LESSON I WIN (Circle one)

HOW DO I FEEL ABOUT IT?

RESOLUTION DATE

KICK-ASS TIP

Having a mentor within your organization is the single-most important strategy for job success, but having a sponsor is the most important factor for career advancement.

YOU ARE **RESPONSIBLE** FOR SELECTING YOUR **MENTORS;** SPONSORS, HOWEVER, BASED ON FACTORS THAT INCLUDE YOUR **WORK PERFORMANCE, CHOOSE YOU.**

I KICK ASS AT WORK!

TODAY'S DATE

CHALLENGE I LESSON I WIN (Circle one)

HOW DO I FEEL ABOUT IT?

RESOLUTION DATE

"IT'S EASY TO **TAKE** IN **INFORMATION,** BUT AT THE END OF THE DAY YOUR CHARGE IS TO **TAKE ACTION.**"

LORI DICKERSON
Fouche, CEO,
Retail & Institutional
Financial Services, TIAA

I KICK ASS AT WORK!

TODAY'S DATE

CHALLENGE I LESSON I WIN (Circle one)

HOW DO I FEEL ABOUT IT?

RESOLUTION DATE

KICK-ASS TIP

DON'T BE **AFRAID OF CHANGE.** FINDING YOUR **NEXT JOB** MAY REQUIRE MOVING TO ANOTHER STATE, A NEW COUNTRY OR **SWITCHING INDUSTRIES.**

I KICK ASS AT WORK!

TODAY'S DATE

CHALLENGE I LESSON I WIN (Circle one)

HOW DO I FEEL ABOUT IT?

RESOLUTION DATE

"BE VISIBLE! NO ONE IS GOING TO **BELIEVE IN YOU,** SUPPORT, OR FOLLOW YOU IF THEY DON'T KNOW WHO YOU ARE."

PATTY AZZARELLO,
Author, Rise:
3 Practical Steps for Advancing Your Career, Standing Out as a Leader, and *Liking Your Life*

I KICK ASS AT WORK!

TODAY'S DATE

CHALLENGE I LESSON I WIN (Circle one)

HOW DO I FEEL ABOUT IT?

RESOLUTION DATE

KICK-ASS TIP

IT'S **IMPORTANT** TO **DEVELOP** A **PROFILE** THAT IS RECOGNIZED BY **SENIOR-LEVEL EXECUTIVES,** BUT KNOW THAT EMPLOYEES AT ALL LEVELS IN AN ORGANIZATION HAVE CAN PROVIDE **VALUABLE INSIGHTS.** ANYONE CAN BE AN ALLY.

I KICK ASS AT WORK!

TODAY'S DATE

CHALLENGE I LESSON I WIN (Circle one)

HOW DO I FEEL ABOUT IT?

RESOLUTION DATE

"Don't wait for review meetings that may only happen twice a year. Schedule regular conversations with your manager to let him or her know what you're doing

AND WHAT YOU'RE **LEARNING** THAT COULD BE **BENEFICIAL** TO THEIR **OBJECTIVES."**

SANDRA SIMS-WILLIAMS,
Chief Diversity Officer, Publicis Groupe

I KICK ASS AT WORK!

TODAY'S DATE

CHALLENGE I LESSON I WIN (Circle one)

HOW DO I FEEL ABOUT IT?

RESOLUTION DATE

KICK-ASS TIP

THE **UNIVERSE RESPONDS** TO **MOVEMENT,** NOT INDECISION. DON'T GET STUCK IN **ANALYTICAL** FEAR AND **DOUBT**. MAKE A DECISION AND **STAND** IN AWE OF THE **SUPPORT.**

I KICK ASS AT WORK!

TODAY'S DATE

CHALLENGE I LESSON I WIN (Circle one)

HOW DO I FEEL ABOUT IT?

RESOLUTION DATE

"For me, the most important thing has always been to get the lesson from every experience. Get the lesson, and then you can move on. Nothing is ever as it appears to be. It shows up in your life for the lesson you were supposed to learn.

WHEN YOU **GET** THE **LESSON,** YOU CAN **MOVE ON."**

OPRAH WINFREY,
Media Executive,
Film and Television Producer

I KICK ASS AT WORK!

TODAY'S DATE

CHALLENGE I LESSON I WIN (Circle one)

HOW DO I FEEL ABOUT IT?

RESOLUTION DATE

KICK-ASS TIP

BEFORE YOU **NEGOTIATE** FOR MORE **MONEY** OR A NEW POSITION, DO YOUR **HOMEWORK** AND KNOW WHAT'S AVAILABLE AND WHAT'S **POSSIBLE,** BUT ALSO KNOW YOUR **NON-NEGOTIABLES.**

I KICK ASS AT WORK!

TODAY'S DATE

CHALLENGE I LESSON I WIN (Circle one)

HOW DO I FEEL ABOUT IT?

RESOLUTION DATE

"There are moments in our lives when we summon the courage to make choices that go against reason, against common sense and the wise counsel of people we trust. But we lean forward nonetheless because, despite all the risks and rational argument,

WE **BELIEVE** THAT THE **PATH** WE ARE **CHOOSING** IS THE RIGHT AND **BEST** THING TO DO."

HOWARD SCHULTZ,
Chairman of Starbucks,
from his book *Onward*

I KICK ASS AT WORK!

TODAY'S DATE

CHALLENGE I LESSON I WIN (Circle one)

HOW DO I FEEL ABOUT IT?

RESOLUTION DATE

KICK-ASS TIP

Be more social. Find ways to connect with your colleagues outside of the office. Join the company sports team, attend your boss' holiday party, volunteer for the company's philanthropic programs.

A LOT OF **IMPORTANT** COMPANY **INFORMATION** THAT MAY BE **HELPFUL** TO YOU IS **DISCUSSED** IN INFORMAL AND **SOCIAL** SETTINGS.

I KICK ASS AT WORK!

TODAY'S DATE

CHALLENGE I LESSON I WIN (Circle one)

HOW DO I FEEL ABOUT IT?

RESOLUTION DATE

"So many people are desperate to find work, that they are more focused on selling themselves to the company than trying to find out if the company is the right fit for them. When you walk away from an interview, you should be able to say,

'**WOW,** THIS IS THE COMPANY THAT **FITS** BECAUSE I REALLY LIKE THE WAY THEY THINK ABOUT **BUSINESS** AND HOW THEIR PEOPLE ARE VALUED.'"

MARLON COUSIN,
Managing Director,
The Marquin Group

I KICK ASS AT WORK!

TODAY'S DATE

CHALLENGE I LESSON I WIN (Circle one)

HOW DO I FEEL ABOUT IT?

RESOLUTION DATE

KICK-ASS TIP

BE **CLEAR** ABOUT YOUR **GOALS.** CLEAR GOALS WILL HELP YOU **DEVELOP** SPECIFIC **STRATEGIES.** YOU CAN'T WING IT.

I KICK ASS AT WORK!

TODAY'S DATE

CHALLENGE I LESSON I WIN (Circle one)

HOW DO I FEEL ABOUT IT?

RESOLUTION DATE

"People skills mean you've taken the time to get to know the inner workings of the people you interact with. You understand their strengths and developmental needs. You understand their natural competencies, and the things that put them outside their comfort zone. When you truly understand your team's skills, then you have the ability, as great leaders do,

TO **GET MORE** FROM THEM THAN THEY EVER THOUGHT **POSSIBLE."**

MARVIN ELLISON,
President and C
EO, JC Penney

I KICK ASS AT WORK!

TODAY'S DATE

CHALLENGE I LESSON I WIN (Circle one)

HOW DO I FEEL ABOUT IT?

RESOLUTION DATE

KICK-ASS TIP

YOU HAVE TO **PLAY POLITICS.** YOU **DON'T** HAVE TO **PLAY DIRTY,** BUT YOU DO HAVE TO PLAY. YOU CAN'T ADVANCE YOUR CAREER AS A DISENGAGED OUTSIDER.

I KICK ASS AT WORK!

TODAY'S DATE

CHALLENGE I LESSON I WIN (Circle one)

HOW DO I FEEL ABOUT IT?

RESOLUTION DATE

"THE **EXECUTION** OF YOUR **PLAN** IS AS **IMPORTANT** AS THE PLAN **ITSELF.**"

JACQUES JIHA,
Commissioner,
New York City
Department of Finance

I KICK ASS AT WORK!

TODAY'S DATE

CHALLENGE I LESSON I WIN (Circle one)

HOW DO I FEEL ABOUT IT?

RESOLUTION DATE

KICK-ASS TIP

Take your vacation. Many employees neglect to take time off for fear of falling behind. The truth is giving yourself a mental break will actually improve your productivity in the workplace.

STEPPING AWAY GIVES YOU TIME TO **THINK,** REASSESS AND **GAIN** NEW **PERSPECTIVES.**

I KICK ASS AT WORK!

TODAY'S DATE

CHALLENGE I LESSON I WIN (Circle one)

HOW DO I FEEL ABOUT IT?

RESOLUTION DATE

"Perception is critical, because it's reality. Your brand represents what you stand for in business and is developed by not just what you say,

CONSISTENCY OF HOW YOU **CONDUCT BUSINESS."**

KEITH WYCHE,
Vice President,
Regional General Manager,
Walmart

I KICK ASS AT WORK!

TODAY'S DATE

CHALLENGE I LESSON I WIN (Circle one)

HOW DO I FEEL ABOUT IT?

RESOLUTION DATE

KICK-ASS TIP

Sometimes a lateral move is better than a promotion. Staying at the same level, but moving to a different division may allow you to develop new competencies that will diversify your skill set.

BROADENING YOUR **EXPERIENCE** WILL CREATE BETTER AND **STRONGER** PROBABILITIES FOR ADVANCEMENT.

I KICK ASS AT WORK!

TODAY'S DATE

CHALLENGE I LESSON I WIN (Circle one)

HOW DO I FEEL ABOUT IT?

RESOLUTION DATE

"Accept what you do does not define who you are. You have to separate your net worth from your self-worth. Your net worth is going to fluctuate—as it should.

THAT'S WHAT **NET WORTH** DOES, BUT YOUR **SELF-WORTH** SHOULD ONLY APPRECIATE."

CHRIS GARDNER,
Entrepreneur and Author

I KICK ASS AT WORK!

TODAY'S DATE

CHALLENGE I LESSON I WIN (Circle one)

HOW DO I FEEL ABOUT IT?

RESOLUTION DATE

KICK-ASS TIP

DON'T IGNORE OR DISCOUNT YOUR **INSTINCT.**

I KICK ASS AT WORK!

TODAY'S DATE

CHALLENGE I LESSON I WIN (Circle one)

HOW DO I FEEL ABOUT IT?

RESOLUTION DATE

"GET ORGANIZED.

IF YOUR MIND ALWAYS SEES A MESS, YOUR MIND BECOMES A MESS."

PEGGY DUNCAN,
Personal Productivity Expert

I KICK ASS AT WORK!

TODAY'S DATE

CHALLENGE I LESSON I WIN (Circle one)

HOW DO I FEEL ABOUT IT?

RESOLUTION DATE

KICK-ASS TIP

MAKE SURE YOUR **LINKEDIN PROFILE** IS A HUNDRED PERCENT **COMPLETE,** INCLUDING A PHOTO. YOU WILL SIGNIFICANTLY **INCREASE** YOUR **CHANCES** TO BE **IDENTIFIED** THROUGH **JOB SEARCHES.**

I KICK ASS AT WORK!

TODAY'S DATE

CHALLENGE I LESSON I WIN (Circle one)

HOW DO I FEEL ABOUT IT?

RESOLUTION DATE

"Unless you're planning to leave your company, you and your boss—whether you like it or not—

WILL HAVE TO **MAINTAIN** A **RELATIONSHIP** THAT YOU CAN INFLUENCE. BE **PERSONABLE**, BUT DON'T TAKE IT **PERSONALLY."**

SANDRA SIMS-WILLIAMS,
Chief Diversity Officer,
Publicis Groupe

I KICK ASS AT WORK!

TODAY'S DATE

CHALLENGE I LESSON I WIN (Circle one)

HOW DO I FEEL ABOUT IT?

RESOLUTION DATE

KICK-ASS TIP

If you are skilled and talented and still believe that working a job you hate is better than looking for a new one, you may have to consider more than your position;

YOU HAVE TO **EXAMINE** YOUR PROFESSIONAL **SELF-WORTH.**

I KICK ASS AT WORK!

TODAY'S DATE

CHALLENGE I LESSON I WIN (Circle one)

HOW DO I FEEL ABOUT IT?

RESOLUTION DATE

"IT'S CRITICAL FOR **YOU AS** AN **INDIVIDUAL** TO REINVENT YOURSELF, TO CONTINUALLY **FIND** NEW **WAYS** OF PROVIDING **VALUE** TO YOUR COMPANY OR **THE MARKET** IN GENERAL."

FRANS JOHANSSON,
Author and CEO of the Medici Group

I KICK ASS AT WORK!

TODAY'S DATE

CHALLENGE I LESSON I WIN (Circle one)

HOW DO I FEEL ABOUT IT?

RESOLUTION DATE

KICK-ASS TIP

Be exceptional in your performance. It's not enough to just satisfy your job description. Find ways to stand out. Exceptional work is what gets recognized,

BUILDS YOUR **BRAND** AS A HIGH-PERFORMING EMPLOYEE AND **LEADS TO PROMOTION.**

I KICK ASS AT WORK!

TODAY'S DATE

CHALLENGE I LESSON I WIN (Circle one)

HOW DO I FEEL ABOUT IT?

RESOLUTION DATE

"'Pray, but when you pray move your feet is an African proverb." I have learned that there is immense value to being still and listening while in prayer. There are times and seasons when waiting is what is being asked of us. But as this proverb infers, prayer also involves response and action. It is powerful to think about what God can do through us as opposed to just 'for us.' Many of us have our personal prayer requests and things that we long for.

WHETHER THEY ARE **SPIRITUAL, PERSONAL** AND **PROFESSIONAL GOALS,** OUR PRAYER MUST BE COUPLED WITH **ACTION."**

NADINE THOMPSON,
President,
Bedroom Kandi Boutique Parties

I KICK ASS AT WORK!

TODAY'S DATE

CHALLENGE I LESSON I WIN (Circle one)

HOW DO I FEEL ABOUT IT?

RESOLUTION DATE

KICK-ASS TIP

Be strategic with all of your social media platforms. Use them as vehicles to brand your expertise, to network and to look for work. If you are out of a job,

LET YOUR **FRIENDS** AND **FOLLOWERS KNOW** YOUR SKILLS AND THE TYPE OF **POSITION** YOU ARE INTERESTED IN ACCESSING.

I KICK ASS AT WORK!

TODAY'S DATE

CHALLENGE I LESSON I WIN (Circle one)

HOW DO I FEEL ABOUT IT?

RESOLUTION DATE

"Don't let your job get in the way of your career. Your job is something you must perform in the moment—it requires a tactical focus. Your career is something you must build over time—it requires a strategic focus. Don't confuse the two.

CORPORATIONS ARE ONLY TOO **HAPPY** TO **ALLOW** YOU TO IGNORE YOUR **CAREER ADVANCEMENT** WHILE YOU SPEND NIGHTS AND WEEKENDS DOING WHAT THEY **NEED DONE."**

RON GOMES,
Vice President Strategic Alliances, HMSHost

I KICK ASS AT WORK!

TODAY'S DATE

CHALLENGE I LESSON I WIN (Circle one)

HOW DO I FEEL ABOUT IT?

RESOLUTION DATE

KICK-ASS TIP

Think creatively, not competitively. When you focus on being competitive, your focus is on being better than the next person. When you are being creative,

YOU **BEGIN** TO **OPERATE** IN A **UNIQUE** SPACE AND GET TO **CREATE** NEW **POSSIBILITIES.**

I KICK ASS AT WORK!

TODAY'S DATE

CHALLENGE I LESSON I WIN (Circle one)

HOW DO I FEEL ABOUT IT?

RESOLUTION DATE

"You don't just play the game on Sunday. You stay in preparation to play the game, so you have to be very disciplined—how you eat, how you get yourself in peak physical and mental condition -

THEN YOU **GO OUT** AND **PERFORM** UNDER PRESSURE AND YOU HAVE AN **END GOAL."**

DON COLEMAN,
Former NFL Linebacker
and Chairman,
CEO of GlobalHue

I KICK ASS AT WORK!

TODAY'S DATE

CHALLENGE I LESSON I WIN (Circle one)

HOW DO I FEEL ABOUT IT?

RESOLUTION DATE

KICK-ASS TIP

EVEN **ADVERSARIES** ARE A **BENEFIT** TO YOU, BECAUSE THEY FORCE YOU—IF YOU PAY ATTENTION—TO NOT BE REACTIONARY, BUT TO BE **REFOCUSED** ON **YOUR GOAL.**

I KICK ASS AT WORK!

TODAY'S DATE

CHALLENGE I LESSON I WIN (Circle one)

HOW DO I FEEL ABOUT IT?

RESOLUTION DATE

"I was one of those people who would knock on your door with the big idea. And the big idea just stayed there. It never got any traction. I got much more introspective and went back to my athletic days where you've got to set goals and measure your progress. It became evident to me that what you do in business is very similar to what I experienced as an athlete. There are no gray areas in athletics.

DID YOU **WIN** OR DID YOU **LOSE?** DID YOU SCORE OR NOT? IT'S VERY MUCH ABOUT **GOALS** AND ACHIEVEMENT."

MATT CARTER,
CEO, Inteliquent

I KICK ASS AT WORK!

TODAY'S DATE

CHALLENGE I LESSON I WIN (Circle one)

HOW DO I FEEL ABOUT IT?

RESOLUTION DATE

KICK-ASS TIP

BE COMPELLING NOT COMPULSIVE. THE FIRST IS **POWERFUL, CONVINCING** AND **CREDIBLE.** THE SECOND IS UNCONTROLLED AND OBSESSIVE.

I KICK ASS AT WORK!

TODAY'S DATE

CHALLENGE I LESSON I WIN (Circle one)

HOW DO I FEEL ABOUT IT?

RESOLUTION DATE

"Success means moving past self-imposed boundaries and pursuing small goals that lead to larger ones. Being successful takes practice, courage and persistence. It requires taking action and prudent risks and

LEARNING FROM **FAILED ATTEMPTS** AS WELL AS **ACCOMPLISHMENTS** ALONG THE **JOURNEY.**"

MARSHA HAYGOOD,
Empowerment Coach,
Author, Motivational Speaker,
StepWise Associates, LLC

I KICK ASS AT WORK!

TODAY'S DATE

CHALLENGE I LESSON I WIN (Circle one)

HOW DO I FEEL ABOUT IT?

RESOLUTION DATE

KICK-ASS TIP

Don't just become a member of a professional organization, consider running for office or volunteering to serve on a task force.

THOSE **ACTIVITIES RAISE** YOUR **PROFILE** AND **STRENGTHEN** YOUR NETWORK.

I KICK ASS AT WORK!

TODAY'S DATE

CHALLENGE I LESSON I WIN (Circle one)

HOW DO I FEEL ABOUT IT?

RESOLUTION DATE

"In the service of being goal-oriented and transactional, we sometimes miss valuable verbal and non-verbal communications. Stay rooted in the personal interaction, experiencing it moment by moment, rather than thinking ahead and anticipating what the person will say next.

YOU WILL BE **BETTER** ABLE TO **LISTEN** MORE INTENTLY AND USE ALL OF YOUR **OBSERVATIONAL SKILLS** TO PICK UP THE MORE SUBTLE **COMMUNICATIONS** THAT MIGHT BE OCCURRING."

BORIS THOMAS,
Psychotherapist and
Executive Coach

I KICK ASS AT WORK!

TODAY'S DATE

CHALLENGE I LESSON I WIN (Circle one)

HOW DO I FEEL ABOUT IT?

RESOLUTION DATE

KICK-ASS TIP

Interview even when you're not looking for a job. It enhances your interviewing skills and helps you gain a real-time assessment of your marketability.

IT WILL ALSO **ALLOW** YOU TO **PRACTICE** YOUR **NEGOTIATING** SKILLS WITH NO PRESSURE TO ACCEPT OR REJECT AN **OFFER.**

I KICK ASS AT WORK!

TODAY'S DATE

CHALLENGE I LESSON I WIN (Circle one)

HOW DO I FEEL ABOUT IT?

RESOLUTION DATE

"The path to a sustainable career—and ultimately life success—begins the habitual practice of wellness as it relates to emotional intelligence, and the time we allot to

THE **DAILY CARE** OF SHARPENING OUR MIND, **FUELING** OUR BODIES, AND **IMPROVING** OUR OVERALL **HEALTH."**

PATRICIA CESAIRE,
Principal Solutions Consultant,
Content Square

I KICK ASS AT WORK!

TODAY'S DATE

CHALLENGE I LESSON I WIN (Circle one)

HOW DO I FEEL ABOUT IT?

RESOLUTION DATE

KICK-ASS TIP

Standing in truth is harder than standing with the group, but standing in integrity is the position that will benefit and reward you in the long run.

IT IS ALSO THE **POSITION** THAT WILL **SATISFY** YOUR **CONSCIENCE.**

I KICK ASS AT WORK!

TODAY'S DATE

CHALLENGE I LESSON I WIN (Circle one)

HOW DO I FEEL ABOUT IT?

RESOLUTION DATE

"During meetings always speak up; whether it's asking a clarifying question or contributing your thoughts and opinions. Never miss an opportunity to let your manager and team know that you are engaged in the discussion.

REALIZE THAT YOUR **PERSPECTIVE** IS VALUED, **APPRECIATED** AND NEEDED. YOUR **CONTRIBUTION MATTERS."**

CECILIA NELSON,
Assistant Vice President
Diversity & Inclusion, L'Oreal USA

I KICK ASS AT WORK!

TODAY'S DATE

CHALLENGE I LESSON I WIN (Circle one)

HOW DO I FEEL ABOUT IT?

RESOLUTION DATE

KICK-ASS TIP

It may seem uncomfortable—and it is often considered taboo, but it's important to talk about salary in safe spaces with mentors, advisors and close colleagues.

IT **GIVES** YOU **PERSPECTIVE** AND A POINT OF REFERENCE FOR THOSE **ADVISING** YOU ON WHAT AND HOW TO **NEGOTIATE.**

I KICK ASS AT WORK!

TODAY'S DATE

CHALLENGE I LESSON I WIN (Circle one)

HOW DO I FEEL ABOUT IT?

RESOLUTION DATE

"**LIFE** IS NOT LINEAR—
YOU HAVE **UPS AND DOWNS.**

IT'S HOW YOU DEAL
WITH THE TROUGH
THAT **DEFINES YOU.**"

MICHAEL LEE-CHIN,
President and Chairman,
Portland Holdings

I KICK ASS AT WORK!

TODAY'S DATE

CHALLENGE I LESSON I WIN (Circle one)

HOW DO I FEEL ABOUT IT?

RESOLUTION DATE

KICK-ASS TIP

Small organizations are great places to start a career. Oftentimes smaller companies operate with limited resources, which requires employees to expand into multiple areas of responsibility.

SMALL COMPANIES ARE **GREAT** PLACES TO **LEARN** AND TAKE **INITIATIVE** ON PROJECTS.

I KICK ASS AT WORK!

TODAY'S DATE

CHALLENGE I LESSON I WIN (Circle one)

HOW DO I FEEL ABOUT IT?

RESOLUTION DATE

"One of the most important lessons I've ever learned was 'speaking into a person's listening.' Successful communication isn't just about what you say, it's about how you say it. Take time to understand your audience's receptivity. Whether you're selling a product, negotiating a contract, managing a team or simply answering an email,

BE INTENTIONAL AND DELIVER A MESSAGE THAT LANDS **ACCURATELY."**

KAREN CHAMBERS,
Executive Vice President,
Impala Inc.,
IMAN Cosmetics and
Jay Manuel Beauty

I KICK ASS AT WORK!

TODAY'S DATE

CHALLENGE | LESSON | WIN (Circle one)

HOW DO I FEEL ABOUT IT?

RESOLUTION DATE

KICK-ASS TIP

If you were to have a brief encounter with someone who could possibly offer you a job, how would you describe yourself? Develop an elevator pitch,

WHICH IS ROUGHLY A THIRTY-SECOND DESCRIPTION OF YOUR **TALENTS, SKILLS** AND **ACCOMPLISHMENTS.**

I KICK ASS AT WORK!

TODAY'S DATE

CHALLENGE I LESSON I WIN (Circle one)

HOW DO I FEEL ABOUT IT?

RESOLUTION DATE

"IF YOU DON'T KNOW THE **FACTS,** DON'T **MAKE THEM UP."**

JUDY SMITH,
Crisis Management Expert

I KICK ASS AT WORK!

TODAY'S DATE

CHALLENGE I LESSON I WIN (Circle one)

HOW DO I FEEL ABOUT IT?

RESOLUTION DATE

KICK-ASS TIP

When researching prospective companies for employment, go beyond the job posting and the website. Research their status and standing in the industry.

IF POSSIBLE, TAP INTO YOUR **NETWORK** FOR INFORMATION ABOUT THEIR **CULTURE** AND HOW EMPLOYEES ARE **TREATED.**

I KICK ASS AT WORK!

TODAY'S DATE

CHALLENGE I LESSON I WIN (Circle one)

HOW DO I FEEL ABOUT IT?

RESOLUTION DATE

"COURAGE IS NOT STANDING ALONE, BUT **STANDING** NEXT TO **SOMEONE** YOU DON'T LIKE TO DO THE **RIGHT THING."**

AMY KLOBUCHAR,
United States Senator from Minnesota

I KICK ASS AT WORK!

TODAY'S DATE

CHALLENGE I LESSON I WIN (Circle one)

HOW DO I FEEL ABOUT IT?

RESOLUTION DATE

KICK-ASS TIP

WORK ON BECOMING AN **EXPERT** IN A PARTICULAR AREA. IT'S GREAT TO HAVE A BROAD RANGE OF **KNOWLEDGE,** BUT EXPERTISE IS WHAT WILL **BUILD YOUR BRAND** IN YOUR **INDUSTRY.**

I KICK ASS AT WORK!

TODAY'S DATE

CHALLENGE I LESSON I WIN (Circle one)

HOW DO I FEEL ABOUT IT?

RESOLUTION DATE

“**INDECISION** IS A **DECISION** THAT ALSO HAS **CONSEQUENCES.** NOT DOING ANYTHING IS STILL A CHOICE.”

JUDY SMITH,
Crisis Management Expert

I KICK ASS AT WORK!

TODAY'S DATE

CHALLENGE I LESSON I WIN (Circle one)

HOW DO I FEEL ABOUT IT?

RESOLUTION DATE

KICK-ASS TIP

LOOK AND **APPLY** FOR **STRETCH** ASSIGNMENTS. THEY ARE PROJECTS THAT ARE OUTSIDE OF YOUR PRESENT SCOPE OF **RESPONSIBILITY,** BUT WILL **HELP** PROVIDE **LEARNING** AND A WAY TO **SHOWCASE** YOUR **TALENTS.**

I KICK ASS AT WORK!

TODAY'S DATE

CHALLENGE I LESSON I WIN (Circle one)

HOW DO I FEEL ABOUT IT?

RESOLUTION DATE

"WHEN YOU'RE NOT **CLEAR** ABOUT WHERE YOU WANT TO GO,

OTHER PEOPLE WILL DIRECT YOUR **LIFE.**"

AUDRA BOHANON,
Senior Partner,
Korn Ferry Hay Group

I KICK ASS AT WORK!

TODAY'S DATE

CHALLENGE I LESSON I WIN (Circle one)

HOW DO I FEEL ABOUT IT?

RESOLUTION DATE

KICK-ASS TIP

BE A **PROBLEM-SOLVER.** THERE ARE ALWAYS NEW AND **IMPROVED** WAYS TO EXECUTE **TASKS, STREAMLINE** PROCESSES, OR ENHANCE PRODUCTION. FINDING WAYS TO BE MORE **EFFICIENT** ARE **VALUABLE** AND QUANTIFIABLE WAYS TO **STRENGTHEN** YOUR **BRAND.**

I KICK ASS AT WORK!

TODAY'S DATE

CHALLENGE I LESSON I WIN (Circle one)

HOW DO I FEEL ABOUT IT?

RESOLUTION DATE

"NEVER COMPROMISE WHO YOU ARE **PERSONALLY** IN **PURSUIT** OF WHO YOU WANT TO BECOME **PROFESSIONALLY."**

JANICE BRYANT HOWROYD,
Founder and CEO,
The Act-1 Group

I KICK ASS AT WORK!

TODAY'S DATE

CHALLENGE I LESSON I WIN (Circle one)

HOW DO I FEEL ABOUT IT?

RESOLUTION DATE

KICK-ASS TIP

Commit to learning everything you can about your role in your industry. Technology, consumer interests and competing companies constantly change the dynamics of the marketplace.

YOU ALWAYS **WANT** TO BE **PREPARED** TO **OPERATE** AHEAD OF THE **CURVE.**

I KICK ASS AT WORK!

TODAY'S DATE

CHALLENGE I LESSON I WIN (Circle one)

HOW DO I FEEL ABOUT IT?

RESOLUTION DATE

"If you start asking what else is possible, it makes it more difficult to turn things into an answer. Even if something shows up that you don't like,

YOU CAN STILL ASK WHAT ELSE IS **POSSIBLE,** SO YOU **START** TO BECOME **AWARE** OF CHOICES YOU MAY NOT HAVE CONSIDERED BEFORE."

RICKY WILLIAMS,
Former American
Football Running Back

I KICK ASS AT WORK!

TODAY'S DATE

CHALLENGE I LESSON I WIN (Circle one)

HOW DO I FEEL ABOUT IT?

RESOLUTION DATE

"The focus needs to be on what I need to prepare myself to participate [in this economy] at a meaningful level in the way that I choose. You don't have to do something new.

YOU **CAN DO** WHAT YOU'VE BEEN DOING, BUT **BETTER, SMARTER** AND WITH MORE **COMMITMENT."**

CHRIS GARDNER,
Entrepreneur and Author

I KICK ASS AT WORK!

TODAY'S DATE

CHALLENGE I LESSON I WIN (Circle one)

HOW DO I FEEL ABOUT IT?

RESOLUTION DATE

MY KICK-ASS ACHIEVEMENTS

This is a dedicated section for you to record your professional accomplishments. This includes actions that have improved operations at work, saved the organization money, gained more customers and solved problems. You will also record any awards, recognitions and milestones you have achieved. These recordings will be instrumental in developing the professional story you share on LinkedIn and on your résumé. It is extremely important to be specific—detailing percentages, revenue and sales numbers, satisfaction ratings and survey scores. When you can quantify your work, you can better describe the impact and significance of your performance.

It is important to note that your manager or company may not acknowledge all of your accomplishments. What's most important is that you recognize and record your professional growth and your contributions to the organization. Your achievements will be part of the story you tell to access your next opportunity.

MY ACCOMPLISHMENT DATE

MY ACCOMPLISHMENT DATE

MY ACCOMPLISHMENT DATE

MY ACCOMPLISHMENT DATE

MY ACCOMPLISHMENT DATE

MY ACCOMPLISHMENT DATE

MY ACCOMPLISHMENT DATE

MY ACCOMPLISHMENT DATE

MY ACCOMPLISHMENT DATE

MY ACCOMPLISHMENT DATE

MY ACCOMPLISHMENT DATE

MY ACCOMPLISHMENT DATE

MY ACCOMPLISHMENT DATE

MY ACCOMPLISHMENT DATE

MY ACCOMPLISHMENT DATE

MY ACCOMPLISHMENT DATE

MY ACCOMPLISHMENT DATE

MY ACCOMPLISHMENT DATE

MY ACCOMPLISHMENT DATE

MY ACCOMPLISHMENT DATE

MY ACCOMPLISHMENT DATE

MY ACCOMPLISHMENT DATE